FLORIDA'S

INCREDIBLE WILD EDIBLES

by

Richard J. Deuerling and Peggy S. Lantz

Cover art and illustrations by Elizabeth Smith

Florida Native Plant Society
P. O. Box 680008, Orlando, Florida 32868

To my wife, Dorothy, who puts up with all my shenanigans. Dick

Acknowledgments

Thanks to Sam Hopkins and Marie Mellinger for the use of their Photographs by the artist; to Helen Dunn Ribbe for typesetting and layout; and to Tony Cavalieri for printing of this publication.

CONTENTS

Foreword, by Marie Mellinger, iv
How to Enjoy Florida's Incredible Wild Edibles, 1

Spring Edibles:
 Salads, 5
 Wild Radishes, 10
 Potherbs, 11
 Poke, 14

Fall Edibles:
 Persimmon, 17
 Sumac: Indian Lemonade, 20
 The Beautiful Beauty Berry, 24
 Acorns, 27
 Nuts to You! 30

Year 'Round Edibles:
 Cattails, the Forager's Friend, 33
 The Pleasures of Sassafras, 36
 Elderberry, 39
 Wild Beverages, 42
 Water Lilies, 49
 Prickly Pear Cactus, 52
 Wild Onions and Garlic, 55
 The Ubiquitous Dandelion, 59
 Potato Substitutes, 62

Index, 67

Foreword

Florida's varying habitats are blessed with a wide variety of native plant species, with roots, stems, leaves, flowers, fruit, and seeds that provide good and interesting food for people. In addition, from the time when the first Calusa aimed his dugout at the Florida coast, and the first Spanish friar planted his mission garden, other edible plants have appeared, brought in by accident or on purpose. Over the years the ever-increasing influx of visitors and residents has added many more edible plant species.

All of these plants, if we are to enjoy eating them, need identification and interpretation, which a book such as this provides. From "Dandelion Dip" to "Elderflower Champagne", Dick Deuerling and Peggy Lantz have found the woods and fields are a table always spread (to paraphrase Thoreau). They take great pleasure in offering accurate descriptions and recipes for Florida's incredible wild edibles.

Marie Mellinger
Author of *Roadside Rambles*

iv.

How To Enjoy
Florida's
Incredible Wild Edibles

Ever since Euell Gibbons in Pennsylvania and Bradford Angier in Canada started spreading the word about edible wild plants, the fun and challenge of reaping where we have not sown has attracted devotees across the country. While it would take too much time and work to sustain yourself and family with edible wild plants unless you had to, as a hobby it is lots of fun, gets one out-of-doors, adds many new plants to your store of knowledge, and puts new flavors on the dinner table.

However, when Euell Gibbons says look for such-and-such a plant to be ready to eat in June, in Florida it might be ready to pick in February! So — as Florida's Chamber of Commerce slogan once said — the rules are different here!

Dick Deuerling knows the rules for finding wild plants to eat in Florida. He has been giving programs on wild foods throughout central Florida for many years. Every month, Dick is on the program of the Tarflower Chapter of the Florida Native Plant Society, sharing his expertise, showing wild plants he has brought to the meeting, and providing refreshments in the form of teas, jellies, and syrups made from wild native plants. He's also a member of the Incredible Wild Edibles, a Georgia-Florida group of wild food enthusiasts.

Dick — brown from the sun, bewhiskered, and often wearing red suspenders — is a self-taught naturalist. He says he has been interested in plants since he could crawl, and has been eating wild foods for fifty years. He grew up in Pennsylvania, and still owns land there, but has lived in Orlando for 32 years — ever since he came to visit a brother and decided to stay.

Teaching came naturally, too, so Dick has shared his information and experiences with many. He has taught survival to Scout troops, and is proud that — of all the Boy Scouts that went on a cross-Florida survival tramp with the late Ross Allen years ago (carrying no food with them) — the Scout that Dick had helped to coach was the only one who gained weight on the 153-mile, thirteen-day hike!

Dick has given wild food programs to practically every garden club in central Florida, including addressing 400 garden clubbers at their convention at a large Orlando hotel. He's shared his pleasure in wild foods with children in public schools and with botany students at the University of Central Florida and Stetson. One group of youngsters at the Orlando Science Center was served a porridge of Jerusalem artichokes and sandspurs — although they were not told what it was until after they had tried it and agreed that it was good!

His schedule includes a TV broadcast with a display of edible native plants, a program for a school science club, and a presentation for the Seminole County Cooperative Extension Service. He is "retired", but very busy.

Dick Deuerling has been "feeding" Peggy Lantz information about edible wild plants for several years, which she has written up and published regularly in the Florida Native Plant Society's magazine, *The Palmetto*. Peggy is also a "weed nut", and has written several articles for other magazines too about edible wild plants. She has been a freelance writer for many years, as well as editor of publications for the Florida Native Plant Society since the Society's founding in 1980. She also served as editor of Florida Audubon Society's magazine, *The Florida Naturalist*, for more than six years.

This book is a compilation of the articles published in *The Palmetto*, with a few new chapters.

Before going out foraging for your first wild edibles, however, you need to be sure you recognize the plants. Some are so easy to identify or so commonly known that you need not worry about picking the wrong plant. Sometimes, though, you need to pick the fresh growth to eat before it reaches the easily recognizable stage. Identifying young sprouts without flowers or seeds to guide you may be a little more difficult. You may have to learn a new plant one year and not sample any of the sprouts until they come up again the following year. If you have a friend who knows the plants and can accompany you a few times, you'll find it more fun and much easier to learn them. Field trips with Florida Native Plant Society chapters are an excellent way to get help.

Gather your newly discovered wild foods and add them to the dinner table one at a time, savoring and experimenting with the new flavors.

It's important to remember that wild foods need to be gathered when they are ready, just as garden vegetables do. Lettuce that has bolted to seed is too bitter to eat. So are wild greens. You pick asparagus when it's only a few inches out of the ground. Similarly, you pick wild poke when it's about eight inches tall. Don't expect old wild foods to taste any better than old garden foods.

On the other hand, don't expect unripe persimmons or nuts to taste any better than unripe oranges or sour apples. Most foods have an optimum time for harvesting.

Wild foods are remarkably nutritious, too. According to the tables in *Stalking the Healthful Herbs* by Euell Gibbons, they compare very favorably with the most vitamin-rich of our cultivated vegetables, and many of them are far superior to the garden varieties. Deep-rooted wild plants bring up more trace minerals from deep in the soil than do shallow-rooted garden plants. Poke, for example, has more than two and a half times as much vitamin C as an orange and more vitamin A than an equal amount of spinach. Wild persimmons have five times as much iron and 35% more potassium than the richest orchard fruit. Most wild greens have incredibly higher amounts of calcium and vitamin A, in particular, when compared to garden greens.

So when you are gathering your spring tonic of wild greens (remember: in January, February, and March, not in June!), you are giving your family a vitamin and mineral supplement.

Can you get your children to eat this stuff? Yes! When the Lantz kids were growing up, they had to put up with all the "weeds" their mother put on the table. They made lots of jokes about it, but they ate it all. Their favorite was cattail blossoms. They would initiate the watch at the pond for the first blossom spikes, and drag out the canoe to gather them.

Most important of all, in all of your foraging, gather your wild foods away from any place where insecticides or herbicides are used, and away from roadways where heavy metals and other pollutants from automobile exhaust settles on plants.

Any requests for special recipes? Or do you have some recipes to share? Or information or questions about other edible plants? Write Dick Deuerling, 5611 Sandalwood Drive, Orlando, FL 32809.

And have a wild time!

Salads

Meadow beauty

Sea rocket

Partridge berry

Spanish needles

Webster's dictionary says a salad is a dish usually made of green vegetables, meats, or fruits, tossed with a dressing. In this discussion of salads, we'll be leaving out the fruits and meats.

The list of salad plants is almost endless. However, we'll have to do some research on them, because most of the descriptions in field guides and identification manuals deal with mature plants. In most cases, this is not what we want for eating. Whether we're foraging for roots such as Florida betony, or shoots such as one of the seven or eight species of *Smilax*, or the leaves of grape vines, we want the very young tender parts for our salads, which often do not look like the mature plant at all.

Peppergrass, for instance, has a rosette of leaves that lies flat on the ground. This is the part we are interested in because it tastes somewhat like water cress. The rosette leaves are smooth and rounded near the center of the rosette and toothed and indented toward the tip of the leaf. After the flower stalk shoots up from the rosette and blooms, its leaves have saw-like edges and are tough and bitter. Then if you wait a little longer until the bloom comes up and seed pods form, these seeds can be stripped off the stem and

Chickweed

Wood sorrel

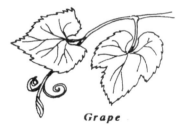

Grape

Peppergrass

sprinkled on top of the salad. Peppergrass also has a beautiful white root that can be ground up and vinegar added to use as a substitute for horseradish.

Some salad greens are mild and bland such as chickweed, dayflower, or purslane. Others, such as peppergrass and water cress, are peppery. Oxalis and sheep sorrel are slightly sour. Some are bitter, such as *Youngia japonica* and dandelion.

To make the salad, gather only what you need just before you want to use it. Otherwise you lose flavor and vitamins and minerals, and end up with something you could get from the supermarket. Mix flavors until you find a combination of strong, mild, sour, and/or bitter that pleases your palate. With a little experimenting, you can make a really good-tasting salad!

Remember, as always: Don't forage along well-traveled roads where plants may have absorbed pollutants from automobile exhaust. If you're gathering plants from natural water bodies and have any doubts about the potability of the water, it might be a good idea to rinse your greens in a pan of water that has about ten drops of an ordinary laundry bleach, in each quart of water. Then rinse the greens in clear water, and pat them dry.

Immediately after rinsing, toss them in a bowl with a small amount of your favorite salad oil (I prefer olive oil). Use just enough to coat them lightly. The oil seals out the oxygen and moisture that depletes the vitamins and minerals. Add vinegar, salt and pepper, more oil if you wish, and any other seasonings you like. Finely chop *Micromeria brownei* — no common name; I call it creeping mint — and add it last of all.

One last caution: be absolutely sure that the plant you're eating is the one listed here. If you're not sure, don't eat it.

A good publication for identifying edible plants when they're immature is *Identifying Seedlings and Mature Weeds Common in the Southeastern U.S.*, by Stucky, 1981. It's published jointly by the North Carolina Agricultural Research Service, Bulletin #461, and the North Carolina Extension Service, AG #208. Costs $5.00 from North Carolina State University, Raleigh, NC.

Sow thistle

Redbud

Daylily

Cleavers

Saw palmetto

FLORIDA PLANTS for SALADS

This list identifies common name, scientific name, edible parts, and, in parentheses, a description of the taste. If the edible part is thᵉ leaves, "young tender leaves" is always implied.

All mints, *Mentha* spp.; leaves (mint).

Amaranth, *Amaranthus* spp.; leaves.

Bear grass, *Yucca filamentosa*; flower petals only.

Bitter cress, *Cardamine pennsylvanica*; leaves, young seed pods.

Bracken fern, *Pteridium aquilinum*; young fiddlehead only (under 2 inches)

Bullrush, *Scirpus validus*; tender young shoots.

Cattail, *Typha* spp.; young roots, shoots (bland).

Chickweed, *Stellaria media*; leaves, stems (bland).

Cleavers, *Galium aparine*; leaves, cooked and cooled.

Creeping mint, *Micromeria brownii*, leaves (mint).

Dandelion, *Taraxacum officinale*; leaves (bitter).

Daylilies, *Hemerocallis fulva*; young shoots, sliced tubers.

Dayflower, *Commelina* spp.; leaves.

False dandelion, *Pyrrhopappus carolinianus*; leaves.

Fireweed, *Erechtites hieracifolia*; leaves.

Florida betony, *Stachys floridana*; sliced tubers.

Glasswort, *Salicornia* spp.; young stem (leaves not present).

Grape, *Vitis* spp.; young, tender leaves, tendrils, (sour).

Greenbriar, catbriar, horsebriar, blaspheme vine, *Smilax* spp. (7 or 8 spp.); young, tender leaves, shoot tips (bland)

Jerusalem artichoke, *Helianthus tuberosus*; sliced tubers.

Meadow beauty, *Rhexia virginica*; leaves.

Mustard, *Brassica* spp.; leaves, young seed pods.

Oxeye daisy, *Chrysanthemum leucanthemum*; petals

Partridge berry, *Mitchella repens*; berries (colorful garnish).

Pellitory, *Parietaria floridana*; leaves (Caution: allergen for some.).

Peppergrass, *Lepidium virginicum*; leaves, seed pods, (peppery).

Pickerel weed, *Pontederia cordata*; leaves.

Plantain, *Plantago major*; leaves cooked and cooled.

Purslane, *Portulaca oleracea*; leaves (bland).

Red bud, *Cercis canadensis*; flowers.

Saw palmetto, *Serenoa repens*; terminal bud (tastier than cabbage palm bud and harvesting does not kill plant).

Sea rocket, *Cakile* spp.; leaves, young seed pods.

Sheep sorrel, *Rumex acetosella*; leaves, seeds (sour).

Shepherd's purse, *Capsella bursa-pastoris*; leaves, seed pods.
Sow thistle, *Sonchus* spp.; leaves.
Spanish bayonet, *Yucca aloifolia*; flower petals only.
Spanish needle, monkey lice, *Bidens alba*; flower petals.
Spiderwort, *Tradescantia ohiensis*; leaves, flowers.
Swamp rose, *Rosa palustris*; petals.
Thistle, *Cirsium* spp.; leaves (spines removed), first-year root.
Violet, *Viola* spp.; leaves, flowers.
Wild garlic, *Allium canadense*; leaves, bulbs, bulblets.
Wild lettuce, *Lactuca* spp.; leaves.
Wild onion, *Allium* spp.; leaves, bulbs.
Wood sorrel, *Oxalis* spp.; leaves (sour).
Youngia, *Youngia japonica*; leaves (bitter)

Spanish bayonet

Oxeye daisies

Amaranth

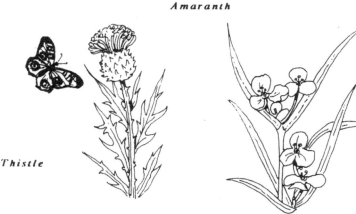

Thistle

Spiderwort

Wild Radishes

Florida betony (*Stachys flori-dana*), sometimes called hedge nettle (though it doesn't seem nettle-y at all) is a member of the mint family — you can tell by its square stem. It has a pinkish-purple flower with dots in the throat. Even Mary Francis Baker,

Florida betony and tubers

the author of *Florida Wild Flowers* published in 1926, said it is edible.

The edible part is a crispy, white, crinkly-shaped underground tuber. They're like radishes without the hot taste, and can be eaten raw, out-of-hand or in a salad, or boiled for a short time in a little water. They also make a very good pickle.

About the end of February, the new year's underground tubers start to form. Tubers from the previous year become soft and mushy as they are used to feed the plant. New tubers are at their best during March and April, and are good through at least May.

The tubers are within a couple of inches of the soil surface, and the plant can sometimes be pulled up with the tubers attached. Digging a little with your hand or trowel will assure a good collection of tubers.

One day, I was presenting a program for a garden club on edible wild plants. The group was standing in an orange grove, nibbling samples of my collection of wild edibles, when one listener complained that they'd never find the species I was talking about. I looked around, leaned over, and pulled up half a dozen tubers of Florida betony, just like the ones I'd brought, already cleaned, for them to eat.

It grows from central Florida north into Georgia and the Carolinas. Let me warn you that Florida betony will take over your yard if it gets started. But if you don't want it there, you can always eat it!

Potherbs

As with the chapter on salads, we'll start with the definition. Webster says that a potherb is "an herb whose leaves or stems are cooked for use as greens." Everyone is familiar with garden "greens" such as spinach, but there is an almost endless list of wild plants that can be cooked and eaten as greens.

Purslane

Perhaps more than with other wild edibles, however, we must be careful about what and how we collect. Most of the guide books and identification manuals show mature plants with flowers and seeds, but with very few descriptions or pictures of new foliage — the part that we now want to know for sure for eating. We want only the very young and tender leaves and stems — just one bad leaf can ruin the whole pot — and a lot of the young edible plants look very similar to ones that are not edible. We want to make no mistakes. Be sure that what you are about to eat is one of the plants that is listed here. If you are not sure, *do not* eat it.

Pickerel weed

The best way to learn is to take an experienced forager or a botanist with you when you go collecting until you can identify the young plants you want to eat. Sometimes, midway through the season, you can find mature plants with blooms alongside still young plants. Then you have the opportunity

White clover

to compare the leaves and be confident of your determination.

More than one kind of potherb can be processed in the same pot at the same time, but they must be heated up hot, hot, hot! Use just enough water to cover the herbs, and bring it to a hard boil. Discard the first water and pour a smaller amount of hot water over the greens. Again bring to a boil, then reduce the heat and simmer until tender — from five minutes to a half hour, depending upon the herb.

Smilax

Some of the herbs in this list are edible without discarding the first water they were boiled in, but for safety's sake, we encourage discarding the first water on all of them to eliminate any undesirable water-soluble agents.

In the case of the more fibrous herbs, a pinch of baking soda may be added to soften the fibers.

After simmering until tender, the potherbs should be chopped up fine or very fine, and seasonings such as salt, pepper, vinegar, cinnamon, or nutmeg added. You may want to add butter, cream, olive oil, or bacon fat with small pieces of crisp bacon. If

Dayflower

you choose, you may flavor with small amounts of wild onion or garlic, or mints. After adding these to the pot, *do not overheat!*

At this stage, you can serve the herbs topped with sliced hard boiled eggs, or put them in a casserole with cheese and bread crumb topping and bake until the cheese melts.

Again, use caution and be sure you have learned to identify the young sprouts of the plants listed here. And, of course, do your gathering in places where pesticides have not been used and automobile emissions have not left pollutants on the plants. Good foraging!

POTHERB PLANTS
(The young, tender leaves are the parts used on each of these herbs. When other parts are also edible, they are added to the description.)

Common name, Latin name, Parts used as well as leaves
Bed straw, *Galium* spp.
Blue lettuce, *Lactuca* spp., buds
Chickweed, *Stellaria media*, stems
Clover, *Trifolium repens*
Curly dock, *Rumex crispus*
Dandelion, *Taraxacum officionale*
Dayflower, *Commelina* spp.
Dollarweed, *Hydrocotyle umbellata*, stems
False dandelion, *Pyrrhopappus carolinianus*
Fireweed, *Erechtites hieracifolia*
Galinsoga, *Galinsoga ciliata*
Greenbrier, *Smilax* spp., shoots
Hawk's beard, *Youngia japonica*
Henbit, *Lamium amplexicaule*
Lamb's quarters, *Chenopodium album*
Mustard, *Brassica* spp., seed pods
Pennsylvania cress, *Cardamine pennsylvanica*, stems
Pickerel weed, *Pontederia cordata*
Plantain, *Plantago major*, leaves stripped of veins
Poke, *Phytolacca americana*, stems under 8"
Purslane, *Portulaca olecacea*, stems
Queen Anne's lace, *Daucus carota*
Redroot pigweed, *Amaranthus hybridus*
Sea rocket, *Cakile* spp., young seed pods
Sheep sorrel, *Rumex acetosella*
Shepherd's purse, *Capsella bursa-pastoris*, seed pods
Sow thistle, *Sonchus asper*
Spanish needle, *Bidens alba*
Spiderwort, *Tradescantia ohiensis*
Spiny amaranth, *Amaranthus spinosus*
Violets, *Viola* spp.
Water hyacinth, *Eichhornia crassipes*
Water pennywort, *Hydrocotyle bonariensis*
Yellow lettuce, *Sonchus oleraceus*

Poke

Mature poke

Poke (*Phytolacca americana*) is another edible plant that has lots of common names, including poke sallet, pigeon berry, inkberry, redwood, scoke, pocan, cancer jalap, garget, ñamoli, pokeweed, redweed, and pokeberry. There are good reasons for all these common names because the plant was well known by different peoples for different reasons — to some it was a valuable edible plant, to others, a medicinal plant, and to still others it was an extremely poisonous plant.

Poke sprouts

It was best known, however, as an edible plant, and it is one of the few that were exported to Europe, mainly France, where it is still cultivated for its edible parts. It was also exported to North Africa. In my travels through the United States on my way home from a six-month camping trip, I went into supermarkets in both Oklahoma and Arkansas where, to my surprise, I found 15-oz. cans of "Griffin's Whole Leaf Poke Salad Greens" for 63¢ a can!

For those who don't recognize this plant, it is a large, rank perennial that grows up to eight or nine feet tall. It can be found in old fields, cultivated lands, fence rows, roadsides, and newly disturbed areas, where it thrives in deep, rich soil.

The leaves are oval to lance-shaped, very smooth, entire (not toothed), with rather long stems that are arranged alternately on the red to purple-colored branches.

The greenish-white flowers arise on six-inch stems opposite the leaves, hanging in racemes in spring, followed in summer and fall by dark purple, slightly flattened berries that are between ¼ and ½ inch in diameter.

The berries contain many small black poisonous seeds. Apparently the Pennsylvania Dutch used the juice and purple pulp of the berries in jellies and pies. It is said that the juice also was used as a food coloring for cake icing. The Portuguese tried using the berries to darken their red wine, but it ruined the flavor, causing the king to order all poke to be cut before it formed fruit. We urge caution in any edible use of poke berries.

Soldiers during the Civil War wrote letters home using the berry juice as ink; hence, the name "inkberry." Some of these historic letters, stored in archives, are still readable to this day.

The mature leaves, and the stems after they have turned red, are toxic. The old timers say that the red color going up the stem is the poison coming up from the roots.

The only edible parts of poke are the new fresh shoots that come up in the spring, before any red comes up the stems. In Florida, that's in January, February and March. They can be recognized when they come out of the ground at the base of the dried red framework of the previous year's plant.

When they are about eight inches tall, snap them off at ground level, leaving all poisonous (emetic) root parts behind. You can cook them with leaves on, or strip the leaves off to cook separately and eat like spinach, while the stems can be eaten like asparagus.

Wash the shoots, be sure all spiders and little creatures are removed, cover with water, and bring to a boil. Pour off the first water, cover again with fresh water, bring to a boil again, and simmer until tender (about six or eight minutes). This may seem like a lot of trouble, but, believe me, it's worth it! But even when you find out how good it is, don't overeat, because too much poke can have a laxative effect on some people.

After cooking, the shoots can be sliced crosswise into half-inch pieces, breaded, fried, and eaten like okra.

A number of greens that come up fresh in the spring about the same time as poke may be used in a combination pot. You may add dock, peppergrass, dandelions, mustards, and other greens to your "spring tonic".

Young poke shoots can also be pickled after being blanched. Pack in sterile jars with a red bay leaf, vinegar, some sugar, mustard seed, and peppergrass seed, if available fresh, or use dried ones from last year. Seal jars and process in boiling water. Allow two months for spices to penetrate the shoots.

You can cultivate poke as well as collecting it wild. Dig the roots after the first cold snap in the fall, cover them with soil, and keep them in a warm, dark place, watering them occasionally. They will send up shoots over and over again all winter for you to harvest and eat.

For those of you who work with dyes, pokeberry is one of the few bright red vegetable dyes available. For more information on dyes and dying, check with your local library; a number of good books are available on this subject.

Persimmon

'"Possum in a 'simmon tree . . ."

Persimmons are so good that, in the Uncle Remus tale by Joel Chandler Harris, Br'er Possum couldn't stop eating them until too late — Br'er B'ar caught him by the tail, stripping all the hair off, which is why Br'er Possum and all his chillun to this day have a naked tail.

Persimmon

Persimmons (*Diospyros virginiana* L.) *are* good, but only when dead ripe, orange in color, and soft and mushy to the touch. Otherwise, they'll really pucker your mouth! They ripen in late summer to late fall and, contrary to rumor, do not need frost to sweeten.

Persimmon trees are common in Florida, growing in dry fields, pinelands, and moist woods, but the very best persimmons I know of grow in the Arbuckle Mountains of south central Oklahoma.

The small (½" to 1 ½") fruits can be picked when they're yellow and will finish ripening off the tree, but they will not get as sweet as when tree-ripened. The trees in Oklahoma bear so many fruits that I shove a limb in a paper bag and shake it to collect the fruit. They don't bear that heavily in Florida, but shaking the tree to make them drop is still the accepted way to collect persimmons.

If some of the crop has already dropped to the ground, be careful when collecting, for the yellow jackets and bees are apt to be eating on them, too.

When you've taken your wild crop home, wash the fruit gently and slip off the cap and stem. Run them through a colander or strainer to squeeze out the pulp. Use the pulp as a topping for ice cream, or make persimmon ice cream.

To make persimmon pancakes, mix a cup of persimmon pulp, 1 egg, 1 cup of flour, a teaspoon of baking soda and a teaspoon of baking powder, and enough milk to make a thin batter. Cook 'em like any other pancakes. M-m-m, good!

Persimmon nut bread can be made using the same recipe as banana bread, substituting persimmon pulp for the banana pulp. Black walnuts are tastier in this recipe than other nuts, and cook it just a little longer than banana bread.

You haven't thrown away the seeds and skins left in your colander, have you? Rinse the seeds off, roast them in the oven at low temperature for a couple of hours, and grind them for a coffee substitute.

Put the skins in the blender, whirl them around a while, and run them out onto a cookie sheet to about ¼" to ½" thick. Bake it slowly in the oven at a low temperature until nearly dry to make "fruit leather".

If you bring home a big crop and haven't time to process them all, you can freeze them whole and work them up later. Or take off the cap, flatten them on a cookie sheet with your hand, and dry them in the sun. When dry, tear them up to remove the seeds, store the fruits and seeds in paper bags (not plastic), and use them as needed.

Not all persimmon trees bear fruit, but even the fruitless ones can provide you with wild tea. Pick mature leaves, and dry them on a tray in the back window of the car (leave the window cracked open for ventilation), or in a gas oven with the pilot light for heat (again, leave the door cracked for ventilation). It takes a couple days to dry them to finger-crispness. The main vein should snap easily when ready. Store them in tight jars in the dark, like any other tea. If they're not dry enough, they'll mold, but moldiness will be apparent: they'll smell and look bad.

Processed and stored properly, the leaves for tea will last at least nine years and probably much longer. At a recent Florida Native Plant Society Tarflower Chapter meeting, I made two batches of tea: one with leaves cured in 1984, one from 1992, without identifying which was which — and members liked the 1984 vintage better! I dry the leaves as above in the gas oven with just the pilot light until they are crumbly dry. I also put the jar and lid in which I will store them in the oven so that they are completely dry. Then I store the jar in a dark, dry place, labeled and dated.

And if your favorite persimmon tree, which is in the Ebony family, should die or have dead branches, the wood is good for carving.

Sumac, the Indian Lemonade

Sumac is a member of the Cashew family. The *Rhus* genus contains several different species and many different common names.

Sumac

Shining sumac (*Rhus copallina*) is the species most likely to be encountered in Florida, for it is the only sumac whose range covers the entire state. It is a small tree or large shrub, with feather-like compound leaves, containing 9 to 21 leaflets with no teeth. It has "wings" on the stems between the leaflets.

Shining sumac is a pretty bush, for its leaves turn bright red in the fall before dropping off for the winter. The flowers are small and yellow-green, borne in clusters at the ends of the branches that bend downwards in fall as the fruit matures.

Fruits are small (about ⅛"), dark red berries covered with hairs. The berries are coated with malic acid, the same chemical that puts the taste in apples. The malic acid is on the outside; tannic acid is on the inside of the berry.

You know the berries are ripe when you can touch your tongue to them (or touch your finger to the berries and then lick your finger) and taste the unmistakable acid taste. Gather the clusters of berries after a dry spell, because rain washes off the malic acid, which is what gives us the taste.

Harvest enough to last for the year by just clipping off the clusters. Store them in a drawstring bag in a dry airy place. I hang mine from the rafters in the carport.

Indian lemonade is made by soaking the berries in hot water from the faucet. Don't use boiling water, and don't wash them or you'll wash away all the goody. Use about two cups of berries to two liters of water. Remove the stems, and soak the berries for half an hour, stirring occasionally. Then strain the juice, to get rid of the hairs, through a couple of layers of cloth — an old sheet, a pillowcase, or a jelly bag, and then a second time through a coffee filter. Add sugar or other sweetener to taste. Presto! Indian lemonade! The Cherokee Indians called it "quallah".

For those who smoke, sumac leaves can be dried and used as a substitute for tobacco.

The only other edible sumac in Florida is *Rhus glabra*, which occurs in a few counties in north Florida. It also has compound leaves with 11 to 25 toothed leaflets, but no wings. Its twigs are covered with a whitish waxy bloom that can be rubbed off. Its fruit is very bright red. The plant ranges up the east coast to Maine and over to Michigan. Its berries can be used the same as *R. copallina*.

If you travel in the fall, you can find sumac as you go. There are other species farther north and out west. Staghorn sumac (*Rhus typhina*), for example, can be found from north Georgia to Maine and Michigan. Its common name comes from the appearance of the winter silhouette of the tree, which looks like a deer's antlers.

It has 11 to 31 leaflets, and its twigs are thick and covered with long, soft, brown hairs. The fruit, as with the other edible varieties, forms in clusters on the ends of the branches, and is dark red.

The only other sumac in the east is fragrant sumac (*Rhus aromatica*). Little is known about this upright shrub, except that it has leaves of three, like poison ivy. The leaves are toothed. It bears red terminal fruits, with a flavor a little stronger than *R. copallina*. It grows in a small area in north Georgia, North and South Carolina, Virginia, and a ways west.

Traveling west, there are numerous small shrubs and trees in this genus, all of which make good lemonade. They all have red berries in terminal clusters and the malic acid taste when you touch them to your tongue. I used squaw bush in Arizona to make a delicious drink.

Sumac is an example of the usefulness of scientific names. In

Florida, *Rhus copallina* is called shining sumac. In the Appalachian Mountains, it becomes mountain sumac. In West Virginia and Pennsylvania, it becomes scarlet sumac. In the northern end of its range in Maine, it is called dwarf sumac or winged sumac. It also

---

Poison Sumac

When I prepare Indian lemonade for programs, a lot of people say, "I thought sumac was poisonous." So we'd better say something about poison sumac.

Only one species is poisonous: *Toxicodendron vernix* (synonym *Rhus vernix*), and it cannot be mistaken for the edible ones. All edible ones have berries in terminal clusters (on the ends of the branches) in some shade of red. Poison sumac has white berries, originating from the leaf axils (where the leaf stems meet the branch) on long-stemmed, droppy, loose clusters.

Poison sumac leaves are compound, as are other sumacs, but with only 7 to 15 leaflets. The rachis (stem to which the leaflets are attached) and the young twigs are red.

Unlike other sumacs, this plant is a wetlands species. Its range is from Orange County north through Florida up to Maine and Michigan.

Touching any part of poison sumac can cause itchy blisters. Even smoke from burning plants is hazardous.

The *Rhus* genus includes *Toxicodendron radicans* (synonym *Rhus radicans*), which is poison ivy. General consensus is that poison oak is a form of poison ivy, not another species. All have the same blistering effect as poison sumac.

---

appears in China and Taiwan, though I can't pronounce the names they use there! But it's still *Rhus copallina* all the way. Linneaus did a good thing when he devised this system. Saves a lot of confusion.

Now for some recipes.

Sumac jelly. It's really easy. The juice is already prepared. Buy a package of Sure-Jell and follow the recipe for elderberry jelly, using 3 cups of juice and 4 ½ cups of sugar. But omit the lemon juice because you want the lemony taste of sumac instead. It makes a fantastic jelly.

Sumac jello. Mix the Indian lemonade, already sweetened, with unflavored gelatin as per the instructions on the gelatin package.

Sumac rubber candy. Bring one cup of Indian lemonade, already sweetened, just to a boil. Add two envelopes of unflavored gelatin, and mix until completely dissolved. Pour into an 8x8 or 8x10 baking pan, and refrigerate for about an hour. Cut and serve. This is an old Girl Scout recipe from my wife.

There are lots and lots of other recipes that can apply here. Be creative!

The Beautiful Beauty Berry

Beauty Berry

Beauty berry (*Callicarpa americana*) is sometimes called beautybush, or French mulberry, another misleading name, for it is neither French nor related to the mulberry (*Morus* spp.).

Some of the other misleading common names of other species are Virginia willow, which is not a willow and not from Virginia; and Jerusalem artichoke, which is not from Jerusalem and is not an artichoke, but a tuberous sunflower! This is why common names cause confusion, and why generic and specific names are important.

In the case of beauty berry, the generic name, *Callicarpa*, comes from the Greek word for beauty. The species name is self-explanatory.

Beauty berry is a deciduous shrub in the Verbena family that grows long stems eight to ten feet tall. For a short while in the winter they drop their leaves and are leggy, but a quick trim after the berries are all gone will entice early new shoots. The leaves are opposite, ovate (egg-shaped), serrate (have teeth all the way around), and light green in color. They are pubescent (hairy) when young and less hairy when mature.

The lilac-colored flowers circle the stems at the nodes in the spring. They're not nearly as noticeable as the bright purple fruits that cluster around the stems just above the leaves late in the summer through the winter. Sometimes as many as twenty or more of the nodes bear fruit. Occasionally I have seen a white-fruited variety.

Beauty berry grows throughout Florida and the southeastern states. It grows best in rich, fertile soils, but will tolerate just about any soil, and likes light shade, but will tolerate full sun.

For many years, the only use I made of the berries was as a thirst-quencher. If the canteen was empty, chewing up and spitting out a berry or two would get the saliva running.

Then about ten years or so ago, I did a program in Orlando at the Twin Tower Hotel and Convention Center for 400 Garden Club members from all over the state. After my talk, in which I mentioned using beauty berries as a thirst-quencher, one of the ladies told me she had been making jelly from beauty berries for many years. I asked her for the recipe and gave her my name and address, but never received it.

Then, just a few years ago when the Tarflower Chapter of the Florida Native Plant Society hosted the Spring Conference in Orlando, I mentioned that I had heard there was a jelly recipe that I had never been able to try.

Betty Kerr, a Florida Native Plant Society member, told me she had it. I offered to give her a stamped, self-addressed envelope if she would send it to me. She turned down the envelope, but within a week had sent me that recipe and several others. I wrote to thank her, and asked permission to pass it on. The berries are so beautiful that they cry out to be made into jelly to decorate the table and your homemade biscuits. She said okay, so here are two of them!

Beauty Berry Jelly

1 ½ qts. beauty berries, washed
2 qts. water
Boil 20 minutes and strain to make infusion.

Use 3 cups infusion, bring to boil, add 1 envelope Sure-Jell and 4 ½ cups sugar. Bring to second boil and boil 2 minutes. Remove from burner and allow to stand until foam forms. Skim off foam. Pour into sterilized jars and cap.

Even Better Beauty Berry Jelly

Follow previous instructions, except use 3 cups infusion plus ½ cup lemon juice, 1 envelope Sure-Jell, and 5 cups sugar.

I have found several places in literature that say that beauty berry is poisonous, though Euell Gibbons' *Handbook of Edible Wild Plants* (co-authored with Gordon Tucker) states, "Growing up in east Texas, we ate these berries freely" without ill effects. But I question whether their taste buds were functioning properly; surely they can't be the same as mine, for I don't find beauty berries very tasty!

The birds, however, *do* like them, especially mockingbirds. We have seen them hanging upside down on the slender, swaying stems to pick off the berries that persist all winter, even when the leaves are gone.

It's a premier Florida native plant, so plant some in your landscape for beauty, for jelly, for the birds, and for the increase of Florida's native species.

Acorns

You don't have to be a squirrel to enjoy the acorns! In fact, acorns provide some tasty treats for us humans.

For foraging purposes, the oaks can be divided into two groups: the white oaks, and the red and black oaks.

Those in the white oak group provide the best eating because the acorns are sweet, not bitter. The white oaks include white oak (*Quercus alba*), live oak (*Q. virginiana*), and swamp chestnut oak (*Q. prinus* or *Q. michauxii*), also known as basket oak or cow oak. These oaks have leaves with round lobes and no prickles on the ends. They set their acorns each year, with acorn meats that are cream-colored and sweet. The inside of the shell is smooth.

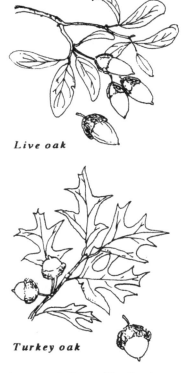

Live oak

The oaks in the black and red group have prickles on the tips of the leaves and take two years to make acorns. The acorn meats are more bitter, yellow to orange in color, and the inside of the shell is tomentose (hairy).

Live oak ranges throughout Florida. The white oak and swamp chestnut oak grow from Alachua County north. These three varieties can be eaten without leaching. Acorns from all oaks can be used for eating, but the tannic acids must be leached out of the black and red oak types. The turkey oak (*Q. laevis*) is purported to be poisonous — some hogs are reported to have died from eating turkey oak acorns — but I have tried them and I'm still alive! They are the bitterest of the bunch, however, and laurel oaks (*Q. hemisphaerica*) are also very bitter.

Turkey oak

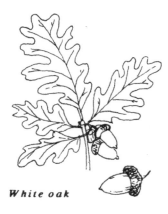

The Indians had a number of ways to leach the tannin out of bitter acorns. Sometimes they put them in a basket and set the basket in a stream for a week or so. Sometimes they just buried them in a swamp, digging them up a month or two later before they started to germinate in the spring. My method is usually to boil them, changing the water a couple times. I usually

White oak

find plenty of acorns from the white oak group so I don't have to bother with the trouble of leaching, but it takes some experimenting to find the sweeter acorns.

Harvesting. When I'm ready to gather acorns (or rather, in the fall and winter when the acorns are ready for me to gather), I have three trees picked out that I have found by experimenting are sweeter than the rest. I gather a bucketful off the ground and tote them home. I fill the bucket with water and throw away any that float. The sinkers I dry out by putting them in a frying pan on

Chestnut oak

the stove. Use a fairly hot heat, but don't roast them. Shake 'em around until they're just dry. Or you can dry them in the oven at 150° to 200° for 15 minutes.

Then crack off the shells with an ordinary nut cracker, or a hammer. Discard the shells and any wormy nuts. You may end up with a quart of nutmeats, depending on the worms.

Flour. Put the nuts in the blender and grind them up. Strain them through a kitchen strainer, and reblend the larger pieces. Now you have acorn flour that you can use in any recipe. Since acorn flour has no gluten, mix it half and half with regular wheat flour to make muffins, pancakes, or quick breads. If it's dried thoroughly, the acorn flour can be stored in tightly capped jars.

Hamburgers. Instead of grinding the nuts into a fine flour, you can chop them into pieces, or save out the larger bits after sifting the flour, to make "hamburgers":

Use ½ cup of coarsely ground acorns, 1 cup of water, some salt, a tablespoon of butter, one large chopped onion, and one egg.

Combine acorn meal, salt, and water in a sauce pan, bring to a boil, and simmer for 15 minutes, covered. Melt the butter in a skillet, add onions and cook until translucent. Then combine the onions, the egg, and the cooked acorn meal in a bowl, add salt and pepper to taste, and mix well. Mold into patties and fry on both sides just like hamburger patties. Add more butter and cover while waiting to serve on a bun with the same condiments you like on hamburgers: ketchup, mustard, relish, mayonnaise, etc. Good as leftovers, too, warmed up.

Microwave acorn candy. Sift a pound of confectioner's sugar with 1 cup acorn flour into a microwave-safe bowl. Put in ½ cup butter or margarine and ¼ cup milk. Heat in the microwave oven until the butter melts (a couple of minutes), then stir until smooth. Reheat slightly if it isn't smooth. Line a tray with plastic wrap, spread the candy over the tray, and cut into squares. Don't make acorn candy if you're on a diet!

Nuts to You!

Florida hosts a large number of native trees with edible nuts. Many of them are partial to the northern part of the state, but enough species grow throughout the peninsula to whet every gatherer's appetite.

Hickories.

Four of the five species of hickory nuts, genus *Carya*, are sweet for eating. The pignut hickory (*Carya glabra*) is the most widespread, covering the whole state except for the southernmost counties. The nut is thick-shelled, and can be sometimes sweet and sometimes bitter.

Pignut hickory

The mockernut (*Carya tomentosa*) grows in the northern third of the state, and does not come as far south as central Florida. The nut of this tree is also thick-shelled and sweet.

Scrub hickory (*Carya floridana*) is not very common, growing in the few remaining undeveloped scrub areas of the central ridge. The nut is sweet.

The water hickory (*Carya aquatica*) is the only hickory with a really bad-tasting, bitter nutmeat. It is edible, however, and not harmful if you like bitter! The nut looks like a pushed-together pecan. Range is all of Florida except for the southern tip, always in wet places, swamps, river edges, etc.

The pecan (*Carya illinoensis*) is, of course, not native to Florida, but to the Mississippi valley. It has escaped from cultivation in some places in the northern part of Florida, and can be planted in yards.

Walnut.

Black walnuts (*Juglans nigra*) are famous for their especially good

taste. The tree grows in north Florida in
upland habitat. The hull makes a good brown
dye, including dying your hands when you
gather them! The local people put the nuts
in the driveway and drive over them to
remove the hull.

Hazelnut.

Black walnut

The hazelnut (*Corylus americana*) is a
handsome tree that grows on the banks of the Apalachicola River in
the Florida Panhandle. It produces an extremely tasty nut.

Chinquapins.

The chinquapins are another group of
small trees that offer nuts to eat. The
Florida chinquapin (*Castanea alnifolia*)
grows as far south as central Florida, with
some found at Wekiwa Springs State Park. It
has a good, sweet, but very small nut, and its
cover has prickles all over it.

The Allegheny chinquapin that grows in
the Panhandle (*Castanea pumila*) also has a
pretty good nut.

Chinquapins

Pines.

Pine trees (*Pinus* spp.) also have edible winged nuts inside the
"scales" of each pine cone. All are edible either roasted or raw (except
for the undesirable invader, the Australian pine, which does not have
cones or edible seeds). The pine tree with the biggest nut is the sugar
pine with enormous seeds that grows in western U.S. The longleaf
(*Pinus palustris*) is the pine in Florida with the largest seeds. It grows
all over the state except for the southeast counties.

Beechnuts.

American beech trees (*Fagus grandifolia*) grow abundantly in north Florida south to Alachua County. The triangular nut has an outside covering with burrs all over it. The nutmeat is sweet, but small, and the shell is hard to remove. The Indians pressed oil from it.

Others.

Basswood (*Tilia americana*) is sometimes called the American linden. Its sweet nuts ripen in the middle of the summer. They are extremely good, but small. They're worth seeking, though, because you can carry a pocketful and pop them in your mouth, bite out the meat, and spit out the shell.

Basswood

The American hornbeam, or blue beech (*Carpinus caroliniana*), has edible nuts, but they're so small they're hardly worth the trouble. Maybe if you're starving . . . The range is from Orange County north.

Key West has planted almond trees in the median of the highway. One time when I was there, the almonds were falling off the trees onto the median strip. I gathered about a bushel of the delicious nuts!

And how can we omit the coconut in a discussion of edible nuts? Of course, the coconut palm (*Cocos nucifera*) is not native, and grows only on the southern shores of the state, but it lacks some of the drawbacks of other nuts — though it's a tough nut to crack, it's very large and its meat is sweet!

Fall is the time to go nutting. So get out there and enjoy!

Cattails, The Forager's Friend

Cattails are the all-purpose plant food. Some folks call it "the outdoor pantry" and "the forager's friend". Cattails also are useful for many purposes other than food. The Boy Scouts say, "You name it, and we'll make it with cattails!"

Cattails

There are three species of cattail and one hybrid: common, or wide-leaf, cattail (*Typha latifolia*), narrowleaf cattail (*T. angustifolia*), and southern cattail (*T. domingensis*), and the hybrid, a cross between wide and narrow-leaf, is *T. glauca*. Fortunately, all of them are edible, so you don't have to worry about differentiating them from each other. You just have to be sure it's not an iris or lily leaf (cattail leaves have no mid-vein, and often last year's old cattails are still evident).

All cattails like wet feet, and grow at the edges of rivers, swamps, streams, and lakes. The best ones are found growing in the mud in shallow water, because it's much easier to harvest the roots, and they'll be cleaner.

Let's start our survey of this incredible edible from the bottom up. The roots contain a flour with a high starch content, derived from the light tan, central core of the root. Preparation is tedious: the root has to be peeled, washed, smashed up in water, the flour allowed to settle, and the fibers removed. Then, a second washing with clean water, another settling and fiber removal. The Indians had a good way of doing it. They used a hollow stump and a rounded stick, which served as a mortar and pestle, to pound the roots. Then they washed the fibers out. When the starch settled to the bottom, they poured off the water and allowed the flour to dry. Cattail flour is excellent, adding good flavor to biscuits, pancakes, and such.

Another part of the root that can be eaten are the small, spaghetti-like spikes that grow around the bottom of the plants. They look like white spaghetti and can be eaten raw or steamed.

The part I like best are new shoots, or rhizomes, that stick out of the root like a round, pointed hook about three or four inches long. This is the start of a new plant. The pure white sprout can be eaten raw, out of hand or in a salad. It tastes a bit like nut-flavored celery, and can also be boiled or baked or pickled. At the right time of year, If I'm on a canoe trip, you could follow my trail by the pulled-up remains of cattails with the rhizomes eaten off.

"Cossack asparagus" is the central core of the new young leaves from the base to about four or five inches up. It is cooked and eaten as a staple food in Russia, which is where it got its name. To eat, pull on the inside leaves until they break loose, then nibble from the bottom up until it's no longer tender.

Another edible part of the cattail is the green flower spike. It comes wrapped in its inner sheath, like corn on the cob. It's cooked like corn, tastes a little like corn, and is eaten like corn. Find them by feeling for the lump in the cattail spike before the brown cattail develops. Peggy and I, after comparing notes on our cattail eating, found that I ate the part of the plant that becomes the brown cattail, while Peggy eats the upper section that turns to yellow pollen. We're both going to try the other's cattail-on-the-cob, and we recommend both parts of the blossom shaft to you. Pick them early, while both parts are still green, and peel off the wrappings. To cook them, add a little salt to some water, add the spikes, and boil them for five or six minutes. Butter them, and nibble the buds off the wiry cob.

Another way to fix them is to scrape off the flowers after they've been cooked, mash them up with butter, and mix them in a casserole with other wild foods.

The upper part, when left on the plant, matures to a bright golden-colored pollen that can also be used to eat. Shake or rub the pollen off into a bag, mix it with flour, and use it to impart a beautiful golden color to biscuits and bread. It's also highly nutritious.

Cattails are useful for purposes other than food. The brown cattail, when mature, goes to fluff that can be used to stuff pillows and mattresses. Back when natural material such as kapok (from a Malaysian tree) was used for life vests and flotation devices, cattail fluff was used when kapok was not available. Brown (but not fluffy) cattails were also used as torches. Dipped in kerosene and lit, they burned for a long time.

The leaves — any species can be used, but the wide-leaf one is best — can be made into placemats, floor mats, and chair seats. Dry them before weaving with them, because the leaves shrink as they dry. Then wet them to make them pliable for working.

It's a diverse plant. It grows all over the United States and Canada, even into Greenland and the Arctic Circle. Its multiple uses for food and products make it truly the forager's friend.

The Pleasures of Sassafras

Sassafras

Sassafras is a member of the Laurel family, which contains such trees as the three *Persea* bays: silk bay, swamp bay, and red bay; camphor and also one shrub: the spice bush. The *Sassafras* genus has only three species in it: one in China, one in Taiwan, and the third — our own United States species, *Sassafras albidum*. Originally, it was named *Sassafras variifolium*, but sometime in the early 1800s it became *S. variifolium* var. *albidum*. Now it's just *S. albidum*. I think the taxonomists should have left it the way it was to begin with, since *variifolium* means "varied leaf" — which it has — while *albidum* refers to "white" — which it appears to not have.

In Florida it grows from Orange County north, where it reaches about 15 feet tall and one to two inches in diameter. It is a large tree in some parts of its range — farther north it increases in size until, in Pennsylvania, it reaches 50 to 60 feet tall and two to three feet in diameter.

In New York State the Indians named it *wah-eh-nak-kas* — their "smelling stick".

At the northern end of its range, sassafras forms small dense clumps, and it's one of the first trees to invade abandoned fields. They don't usually form pure stands, but grow in association with dogwood, American hornbeam, oak, persimmon, and others.

The leaves are unique and unmistakable. They are 3" to 5" long, and 1 ½" to 3 ½" wide. They come in three shapes: entire (which means not lobed at all), mitten-shaped (either left or right), or three-lobed. Sometimes all three shapes are on one twig, sometimes they are scattered all over the tree. In one case on I saw a tree with all its leaves entire. And I also have collected one five-lobed leaf. Indian lore says that it's good luck if you find a matched mitten pair, one left and one right, on the same tree.

The leaves are deciduous, turning yellow and red in the fall before they drop off.

Both leaves and twigs are aromatic with that wonderful, special sassafras odor. And yet on one occasion I found a sassafras tree with no aroma at all. On a canoe trip with my (then) nine-year-old son, I told him to pick and crush the leaves from a tree with three-lobed leaves and smell them. He couldn't smell anything — and when he handed them to me, neither could I! I've never encountered this phenomenon again, but I guess it happens sometimes.

The flowers are yellow-green, and bloom about the same time that the leaves appear in spring. Male and female flowers appear on separate trees. The fruit is a round, blue-stone fruit (drupe), with an orange-red cap and a long stem, and with very aromatic flesh.

The wood is light, durable in contact with soil, and orange-brown in color. It, too, is slightly aromatic. One of my hiking sticks is made from this wood.

The sassafras appears in well-drained soils in fence rows and fields. It is one of the few plants that have been introduced from the New World to the flora of Europe.

Now we get to the good part — how to prepare it to eat.

Sassafras tea has long been known as a spring tonic. Tea is made from the roots, either from suckers or from a tree. Digging and clipping a few roots off a tree will not hurt it. Pack the dirt back around the cut to eliminate air, and it will heal. Wash the roots, break them up or sliver them, and boil for a few minutes in water. They can be saved, dried, and used over again.

You can even buy it bottled now in some of the supermarkets. It goes by the name of Pappy's Sassafras Concentrate Instant Tea. If you mix a bottle of this concentrate with a gallon of cider or apple juice, you come up with a delicious "sassy-apple" drink!

You can make a similar tea from roots of the camphor tree, which has an aroma similar to sassafras, but it's not nearly as good.

The dried crushed leaves of the sassafras are the "filet gumbo" in Cajun cooking. You can use powdered leaves as thickener in all soups and stews.

Sassafras makes a delicious jelly. Brew three cups of strong tea and make jelly following the recipe on a box of Sure-Jell.

Once you've made the jelly, use it in your baking. Make up a cookie recipe, put dabs of the dough on a cookie sheet, press a hollow in the cookie with your knuckle, and fill the hollow with jelly before you bake them. You'll have cookies with sassafras jelly filling.

Or cut small triangles from bake-and-serve croissants, and fill them with jelly before baking, or make sassafras jelly-filled doughnuts. Use your imagination and creativity, and let me know if you come up with something good.

Beer can be made by boiling sassafras twigs in water, adding molasses, and letting it ferment. Filter and bottle.

There has been talk lately about sassafras and other herbal teas being carcinogenic. I feel it's doubtful. You probably couldn't ingest enough even over a long period of time to be harmful. But be sensible: don't steep or boil teas for long periods of time. Brew them just enough to make a good-tasting tea.

Elderberry

By its Latin name, *Sambucus canadensis* (or *Sambucus simpsonii*), you can tell that elderberry ranges far and wide, north to Canada and west to Louisiana. The northern elderberry loses its leaves in winter, while *S. simpsonii* is evergreen,

Elderberry

blooming and bearing fruit almost year-round. It likes dampness, growing along canals, roadside swales, and lake edges.

It is easy to recognize, growing to ten feet high, with compound leaves, five-inch lacy clusters of small, white blossoms in an umbrella shape, and umbrellas of small, black berries. In Florida, you can often find blossoms, green berries, and ripe black berries on the same bush at the same time.

Both blossoms and berries provide wild-food delectables. Pick full heads of blossoms, dip them in batter, and fry them in deep fat. Then eat them right off the stem.

Or pull the blossoms off the stems and mix them in the batter before you cook pancakes. If you smell the delicate odor of the blossoms, you'll get an idea of the flavor that will be added to your breakfast pancakes.

To make a hot tea from dried elder blossoms, pick and shake the blossoms off the stems (be sure all the stems are removed because they add a rankness to the flavor) onto a cookie sheet, leave in the oven with pilot light or oven light on (but no other heat) until thoroughly dry (a couple of days). Store in a closed bottle in the dark, and steep as you would any other tea, using a teaspoonful of dried blossoms and boiling water. Tea can be made from fresh blossoms, too.

The prettiest and tastiest syrup and jelly you ever had can be made from the ripe berries. Pick a grocery bagful of bunches of the black berries, rinse the dust off, strip the berries off the stems, and boil gently in a little water, mashing the berries as they soften. Strain through a cloth as you would any jelly. Add sugar equal to the amount of juice and — to make syrup — boil until the sugar is dissolved.

To make jelly, add a package of commercial pectin such as Sure-Jell to the juice and sugar, and follow directions on the package, which calls for lemon or apple juice to add some tartness. Or make it "straight", which I prefer, though it has to be cooked a little longer to jell.

You've heard of elderberry pie? Make it from fresh, frozen, or reconstituted dried berries. Add an equal amount of sugar, then add a tablespoon or two of both corn starch and water. Pour the mixture into a pie shell, cook, and eat.

Try this idea for more elderberry goodies. Buy refrigerator croissant rolls, flatten them into long shapes on a cookie tin, and turn up the edges (to hold in the juice). Spread on elderberry pie mixture and bake until golden brown and bubbly. No samples of this recipe have ever come back home from a Florida Native Plant Society Tarflower Chapter meeting!

If you're into this hobby for the long term, try brewing some elderberry wine from the berries, or champagne from the blossoms.

CHAMPAGNE from ELDER BLOSSOMS

Ingredients: Sugar, 3½ cups

                      Lemon, 2 small or 1 large

                      Elder blossoms, 4 or 5 large umbels in full bloom

                      Vinegar (white), 2 tablespoons

                      Water (cold), 5 liters

Equipment: A large crock, jug, or glass bowl (large enough to hold about 6 liters)

                      5 clean, 1-liter, screw-top, plastic bottles, or champagne bottles

Method: In large crock, dissolve the sugar in a small amount of warm water and *let cool*. Wash and cut the lemon in half, squeeze juice into sugar solution, then cut the rind into small pieces and add to crock. Remove large stems from elder blossoms and add blossoms to crock. Now add vinegar and cold water. Mix well, and let stand for 4 days to ferment, then strain through muslin (or other cloth) and bottle in screw-top bottles. Will be ready to drink in 6 to 10 days. Enjoy!

Wild Beverages

Tired of coffee? Too much caffeine? Why not try making your own teas and coffee from wild plants? You can brighten your day and sweeten your palate with a new taste treat by doing it yourself! Hollies, wild mints, the persimmon tree, and even goldenrod brew up interesting and delightful beverages.

Hollies

The various species of holly leaves must be dried and then roasted until golden brown before steeping. Hollies and the four "coffees" described are the only ones that require roasting to finish the drying process.

Dahoon holly

Yaupon (*Ilex vomitoria*) has the highest caffeine content of any North American plant. It was the source of the Indians' infamous "black drink", which they prepared by boiling it to excess, and then they drank it to excess, causing — true to its botanical name — all manner of ill after-effects. It makes a good tea if the leaves are steeped for just six or seven minutes without boiling them, but don't use yaupon if you're trying to brew a non-caffeinated drink.

Three other hollies make good tea without the caffeine: Dahoon holly (*Ilex cassine*), American holly (*Ilex opaca*), and Gallberry (*Ilex glabra*). Prepare them all by drying them, then roasting them in a slow oven until golden brown, then steeping them in boiling water.

Since American holly is frequently used to make Christmas wreaths, recycle your wreath after the holidays by making tea from the leaves!

All of the rest of the teas described here need only be dried for brewing and storing.

Mint

Any plant that smells like mint when crushed and has a square stem is acceptable for making tea (all mints have a square stem, but not all square-stemmed plants are mints, so use both tests). Some of the mint leaves can be used fresh as well as dried. Use two teaspoonsful to make a cup of tea from fresh leaves, and one if the leaves are dried.

You know two of the best: spearmint (*Mentha spicata*) and peppermint (*M. piperita*). Others are good, too: *Micromeria brownei*, henbit (*Lamium amplexicaule*), ground ivy, also called gill-over-the-ground (*Glechoma hederacea*), pennyroyal (*Hedeoma pulegioides*). False pennyroyal (*Piloblephis rigida*) is a woody mint; you can brew leaves and blossoms and stems, too.

False pennyroyal

Goldenrod tea

One variety of even the notorious goldenrod can be used for tea. The species is called sweet goldenrod (*Solidago odora*) and only this one out of about 25 in Florida makes a good tea. It can be recognized because its leaves have translucent spots on them, and when crushed they smell like anise. Sweet goldenrod tea, marketed as "Blue Mountain Tea", is one of the few edible wild plants that have been exported.

Blackberry tea

The leaves of all the various blackberry and dewberry types (*Rubus* spp.) are good for tea, and also can be used medicinally for relieving diarrhea.

Blackberry

Violet tea

The leaves of all the native violets (*Viola* spp.) (but not African violets) make good tea. (You can also use the leaves fresh in salads or cooked like spinach.)

Clover tea

The dried blossom heads of some of the clovers can be used for tea: white clover (*Trifolium* spp.) and red clover (*Trifolium prayense*). (Clovers are not native plants, but are escaped from cultivation, so take your vengeance upon them by drinking them!)

Violet

Sassafras tea

Sassafras (*Sassafras albidum*) tea is made from the boiled bark of the roots of the tree. The roots may be boiled several times before they will no longer produce any color or flavor. And you can now buy "Pappy's Sassafras Concentrate Instant Tea" in your supermarket!

A similar-tasting tea can be brewed from the roots of camphor trees (*Cinnamomum camphora*), but it's not as good.

And the dried, crushed leaves of sassafras are the "filet gumbo" in Cajun cooking.

Sumac lemonade

Sumac (*Rhus* spp.; *Rhus copallina* is the species most often encountered in Florida.) makes a drink that tastes something like lemonade. Don't be afraid of collecting poison sumac (*Rhus vernix*) by mistake, for the poisonous variety has white or greenish berries, and the flower cluster comes from the laterals rather than the terminals. Drinkable sumac has blossoms on the ends of the branches and red berries, and all varieties of sumac with red berries are good to use. After berries develop and become red, harvest before it rains. A hard rain will wash off the coating of malic acid (contained in the juice of apples, too) which gives it the flavor for the drink. Don't wash the berries, either, for the same reason. Fill a container with enough hot water from the tap (do not use boiling water because the berry contains bitter tannin, which would be released) to cover the berries, and mash

MAKING TEA FROM WILD PLANTS

Teas can be made from the leaves of many different plants. The leaves should be picked when mature — not too young and not too old. Some can be used fresh, but most should — and all can — be dried before using, and can be stored in a dark place in tightly capped jars. I store my jars on special shelves built for that purpose and shielded with a cover to stay dark.

To prepare, wash the leaves, spread them out on cookie sheets, and set them in the oven. If you have a gas oven, just leave on the pilot light and crack the door open with a pencil to let out the moisture. If you have an electric range with an oven light that stays on when the door is open, the light may provide enough warmth to dry the leaves. Again, open the door a crack for air circulation. Leave them overnight, or until they will crumble dryly in your fingers.

You can also lay them on newspapers and cover them with a newspaper, then put them on the back shelf of your car while it sits in the sun. Open the window a crack to let out moisture, and leave them there all day to dry.

Don't over-dry, or you'll lose the volatile oils that make the flavor in your tea. Properly dried leaves can be kept safely for a long time in tightly capped bottles. Improperly dried leaves can mold. Moldy leaves will look and smell bad. Do not use them.

To prepare a cup of tea, put a teaspoon of your dried leaves in a cup, or one teaspoon per cup in a pot, and add boiling water. Steep for about six minutes. Don't steep too long. The tea tastes best if you drink it right after making it, without letting it stand for any length of time.

Try the tea unsweetened or sweeten it with sugar, honey, or artificial sweetener until it suits your palate.

them with a potato masher or rub them together with your hands. Strain the juice through a pillowcase, muslin bag, or coffee filter to remove the tiny hairs. Just hang the bag over a pitcher and pour the juice through it. (Then plant the seeds. You haven't hurt them because you didn't use boiling water.) Sweeten the drink with honey or sugar. (See chapter on sumac for more information and recipes.)

Rosehip tea

If you have any roses around — wild or cultivated (*Rosa* spp.) — the fruits, called rosehips, make a good tea. (Be sure to avoid any cultivated roses that have been sprayed or dusted.) Pinch off the bitter blossom end, dry them, and store them whole in a jar. When you're ready for a cup of rosehip tea, put them in a blender and start and stop the blender a few times to chop the hips into bits without grinding them to mush. Then pour boiling water over a teaspoonful of them in a cup, and let steep for five or six minutes. Strain, sweeten, and drink. Rosehips are very high in vitamin C, surpassing orange juice.

Wild rose

Yarrow tea

In the northern part of the state, you can make tea from the leaves of yarrow (*Achillea millefolium*). Dry them and steep them as described, but use a little less than one teaspoon per cup.

Chufa tea

Yellownut sedge (*Cyperus esculentus*), also known as chufa, nut grass, or earth almond, has tubers that can be eaten out of hand, roasted and ground to make a coffee substitute, or mashed and made into flour. The tubers can be made into a good drink by mashing them, adding water, and letting the mixture set for a couple of days. Then strain it through a cloth.

Pine needle tea

Pine needles from all kinds of pine trees (*Pinus* spp.) make a different and delicious tea. It's the easiest tea to make — needs no drying. Just pick a few fresh young tender needles, cut them up into small pieces, pour boiling water over them, let steep, strain, and drink. You can do the same with other conifers, arbor vitae, hemlock, spruce, fir, and red cedar.

Longleaf pine

Basswood blossom tea

Basswood (*Tilia americana*) blossoms, as well as winter buds, picked and brewed fresh, make a delicate tea. Ground-up fruits and blossoms, crushed in a mortar and pestle, make a chocolate substitute (it must be used immediately, for it does not keep). The blossoms can be dried and stored in capped bottles for future use, too. Basswood nuts are good to eat out of hand.   Put the

Basswood

whole nut in your mouth and crack the cover with your teeth, eat the kernel and spit out the cover. The sap of the basswood tree is sweet, and can be tapped and boiled down to syrup, like the sap of the maple tree.

Elder blossom tea

Elderberry (*Sambucus canadensis*) offers three fantastic drinks: elderberry wine from the berries, and both tea and champagne from the blossoms. (See chapter on Elderberry for more information and recipes, including champagne instructions).

Persimmon tea

Persimmon (*Diospyros virginiana*) tea, made from the dried leaves of the persimmon tree, also tastes similar to sassafras.

Mexican tea

Mexican tea, also called wormseed (*Chenopodium ambrosioides*), is not my favorite, but packages of leaves can be found for sale in markets in the southwest part of the U.S.

Coffees

Coffee substitutes can be made from the root-nuts of chufa, also called yellow nut grass, (*Cyperus esculentus*, an Old World native plant) persimmon seeds, dandelion roots (*Taraxacum officinale*, from Eurasia), or chicory roots (*Cichorium intybus*). Roast them until they are brown clear through and will crack in your hand, then grind in the blender or coffee grinder to the same coarseness as your regular coffee. Do not overbrew!

Candy

If you have some left-over mint leaves, clover blossoms, or violets after you've dried all the tea leaves you want, make candy. Wash the leaves or blossoms and pat them dry. Separate an egg and beat the white a little, paint the whites on the fresh leaves or blossoms, then sprinkle them with granulated sugar. Turn the pieces over, clean up the sugar that fell off, and sprinkle again, until the egg white won't hold any more. Let dry, and refrigerate or freeze.

Water Lilies

Three of the beautiful and common water lilies that grow in Florida's quiet waters — streams, ponds, and lakes — can be included in your pantry of edible wild plants.

Water lilies are in the family Nymphaeaceae, named for the water nymphs of Greek mythology. The three edible water lilies are the American lotus (*Nelumbo lutea*), the fragrant water lily (*Nymphaea odorata*), and the yellow pond lily (*Nuphar lutea*).

The American lotus is also called the yellow lotus, lotus lily, nelumbo, and water chinquapin. It grows in quiet waters at depths of three to six feet. It has pale yellow, waxy flowers, six to eight inches in diameter, that bloom above the water on long stems from July to late fall. The leaves are huge — a foot in diameter — and bowl-shaped, and are also carried above water.

Lotus

The petiole of the leaf stem is attached to the center of the leaf.

The unopened young blossoms and still-curled leaves are good to eat. Pick them when they're still under water only a few inches off the bottom. They can be boiled and buttered, or added to soups and stews.

The seed pod looks like a shower head, and is frequently included in winter bouquets, sometimes painted or gilded. The pods ripen in summer to autumn. The unripe seeds can be boiled or roasted. The ripe seeds, however, are very hard, and must be roasted and cracked. They can then be eaten like chestnuts, and they taste a bit like them, too. The roasted seeds also can be ground into flour and added to other flours for breads, muffins, and cookies.

The root is good to eat, too, though it's a little harder to gather since it's in three to six feet of water! Dig them with a potato fork, which has curved tines. Harvest the crisp tubers from fall to spring, boil or roast them, and eat them like sweet potatoes.

The fragrant water lily is also called the white water lily, and grows in the same quiet-water habitat. It flowers from March to late fall — white, with a yellow center and petals that taper at the tip. They smell too good to eat! But they are tasty, and there are

Fragrant water lily

plenty, plenty, plenty of them, so enjoy with no sense of guilt.

Gather the unopened flower buds that are still close to the bottom on three to four-inch stems, cook them for two or three minutes in boiling water, and serve with butter. Or saute them in butter. Or, as with other foods, wild or cultivated, they can be added to soups or stews.

The leaves, five inches across, lie flat on top of the water, like a dinner plate with a wedge cut out where the stem is attached. They are dull green on top, purplish underneath, and are edible when they are still underwater and just beginning to uncurl. Cook them in salted water eight to ten minutes.

The seed pods mature underwater, and though I understand they're edible, too, I have never tried them.

The yellow pond lily is also called spatterdock, cow lily, yellow water lily, and water collard. The habitat is the same as the other lilies, plus it can be found growing in swamps.

It blooms from May to late fall. The flowers have fleshy petals

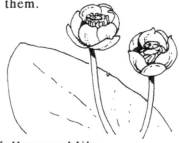

Yellow pond lily

and look like yellow golf balls. Nothing else in the water looks like it.

The leaves are oval, fleshy, notched at the base, and large — 9 to 15 inches across. Unlike the others, these leaves don't lie down flat, but curl up out of the water.

The foot or so of the terminal end of the fleshy rhizome is the edible part. Quarter-inch round roots anchor it to the bottom, and the whole system could be as big as my leg. Gather the rhizomes from fall to spring when they're full and crispy. They get mushy and soft in the summer, when blooming is taking its stored nourishment, but in fall when the blooming and seeding is over, the plant begins to replenish its starch. The rhizome fills out and becomes crispy. Scrub the gathered roots and cut them up. Add them to soups and stews, or boil or roast them for 25 to 30 minutes. They can also be dried and ground into flour.

The seeds are probably the best part. The seed pod is urn-shaped, and yellowish green, tinged at the top with red. A row of spurs protrudes from the bottom around the stem. Harvest the seed pods in the fall when they are ripe. Dry them, and open them up and remove the BB-like seeds. They pop like popcorn — perhaps not quite as well as Orville Redenbacher's, but they pop pretty well, and they are tasty.

The seeds can also be parched over slow heat in a skillet. This releases the outside of the hull, which can then be winnowed to remove the hulls. Then they can be cooked like rice or ground into flour. These are very, very good.

Prickly Pear Cactus

The prickly pear cactus (*Opuntia* spp.) seems an unlikely native plant to provide delicious wild foods. But it does!

Not long ago I took a fall trip out west through the Big Bend area of Texas. I stayed overnight at a campsite that was full of

Prickly pear cactus

Opuntia englemanii that made a barrier around the campsite. The fruits were big and ripe and dropping off on the ground, so — though one is not supposed to take any growing things from a national park — I let a few of them drop into my pot, and made a delicious drink.

I usually pick prickly pears in February, but often there are two fruitings, and I see prickly pears that ripen in the fall. Wait until the pears are nice and red on the outside and will drop off when grasped with kitchen tongs and given a half-turn.

You can find prickly pears and pads in many supermarkets now, catering to the Latin American trade: Goodings, Publix, Xtra. But they also grow all over the dry places in Florida, from sand dunes to dry woods.

The pear-shaped, usually red, fruit that forms after the yellow flower falls off makes one of the best drinks you can imagine. I harvest it by the five-gallon bucketful. Take along kitchen tongs to help you avoid the spines. The big spines are fairly easy to avoid, but the tiny spiny glochids are hard to see and can stay stuck in your skin for a week. Handle with tongs and care.

When I get the bucketful home, I wash the pears in a screen box with a hose on high pressure. This washes off most of the glochids and they wash through the screen. Then take them into the kitchen. I recommend you still handle the pears with tongs while you cut the fruit lengthwise, and slide the pieces off the end of the cuttingboard into a five-quart saucepan. Add a couple cups of water and simmer twenty to thirty minutes or so until they become mushy, then mash them with an old-fashioned potato masher.

Lay a double thickness of a good-sized piece of unbleached cotton muslin (or a pillowcase or piece of sheet) in a stainless steel bowl, put the cooked fruit in it, pull the corners up, and tie them with a string. Hang the bag up over the bowl, tied to the cabinet knob or a cup hook, and let it drip. The juice will be a beautiful clear red. If you don't mind the slight loss of clarity, you can squeeze the bag to get more juice out after it's cool enough to handle.

From this point, you can make a juice drink, syrup, jelly, or candy, depending on whether or not you include commercial pectin and how long you cook it.

To make a delicious cool drink, add two cups of water to two cups of juice, and add honey or sugar to taste. If you like, you can add orange juice or lemon.

To make syrup, just add honey or sugar, and boil lightly.

To make candy, add sugar, cook it until it sheets off the spoon, then pour it in drops on a lightly greased cookie sheet. When cool enough to handle, roll into balls in powdered sugar.

Make jelly by adding commercial pectin, such as Sure-Jell. Use one of the recipes on the package, substituting cactus pear juice. Add sugar and cook it, following the directions.

To save the juice and prepare it later, measure off two cups into quart-size freezer Ziplock bags. Zip them tight, lay them flat on a tray, and put them in the freezer to use whenever you find the time. Be sure to put the date on the bags.

Now, don't waste the seeds! The Indians ground them into flour. Wash away the pulp, and grind the light tan seeds in a grinder or the blender, and add them to pancakes or biscuits, or thicken soup with it.

The pads — or ears, as some call them — are also edible. Use fresh, new pads, and, again, use tongs to hold them with while you cut them off, carefully avoiding the spines and the tiny glochids. Cut out the "eyes", where the thorns grow, with a knife, just as you would the eyes of a potato. Then you can peel them by scalding them in boiling water for one minute and slipping the skin, or you can leave the thin, edible peel on. Slice the pads up like French-cut beans, and simmer them in a little water for five or ten minutes until tender. Add salt to taste. Or dice them and put them in scrambled eggs. Or stew them with crisp bacon, sauteed onions, sweet red pepper, tomatoes, salt, oregano, thyme, and pepper, with bread crumbs and parsley on top.

Or experiment with your own ingenious recipes.

Wild Onions and Garlic

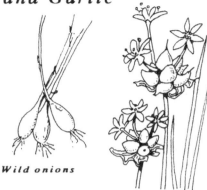

Any plant that smells like onion or garlic is good to eat. If it looks like onion or garlic — but doesn't have the odor — beware of eating it.

Onions and garlics belong in the Lily family. The most common edible species is *Allium cana-*

Wild onions

dense, sometimes called meadow garlic as well as wild onion. It has flattened solid leaves instead of hollow tubes, and the spathe is at the top of a pith-filled, round tube that may carry just bulblets, or may have bulblets with pinkish-white flowers, or may have sprouted bulblets with green tails.

All parts of the onion are edible — the underground bulbs, or the long, thin leaves, or the bulblets on top. Spring is the season — before flowering — to use them as you would green onions. If you want to use the best bulbs later in the summer or fall — they'll be like little pearl onions — you have to know where the plants are before the tops die back; in late summer the whole plant becomes dormant, and there will be nothing left on top to show you where to dig! These are the bulbs I use for pickling. They are about six inches deep, so you need to do a lot of finding, digging, and cleaning, but it's worth it.

I don't buy anything from the store except the vinegar. I use two red bay (*Persea borbonia*) leaves in each jar. I use the seeds of peppergrass and wild mustard. And I never can make enough to last the year!

You can use them like green onions before the flower stalk shoots up, or dig the bulbs at the time when the tops shatter and the bulblets break up and fall to the ground, or you can eat the bulblets. Or pickle them.

Or plant them and make an onion patch of your own somewhere in the back yard. Onions propagate by splitting the underground bulb, or by the bulblets on top falling to the ground and starting new plants. Garlic sets produce "toes" on the sides of the underground bulb and sometimes bulblets on the top. You can propagate onions in your own yard by scattering the bulblets off the bloom, or by transplanting the underground bulbs.

Wild onions can be substituted in any recipe that calls for grocery store onions. Here are a few especially for the wild ones.

Pickled Onions
    1 ½ qts. wild onion bulbs
    ½ cup salt
    1 ½ cups granulated sugar
    1 ½ Tbsp. mustard seed, either wild or from the store
    1 ½ Tbsp. peppergrass seed
    2 bay leaves per ½ pint jar
    4 ½ cups distilled vinegar
Scald onions in boiling water for 2 minutes, then quickly dip in cold water. If any skins are loose, peel them off.

Put onions in a glass, stainless steel, or enamel bowl. Sprinkle with salt. Cover with cold water, and let stand for 12 hours. Then drain, rinse, and drain again.

Combine sugar, mustard seed, peppergrass seed, and vinegar, and simmer for 5 or 6 minutes.

Sterilize jars. Pack onions in the clean hot jars. Add 2 bay leaves to each jar alongside the onions. Pour hot liquid over top to within a half inch of top, covering all onions. Cap immediately, using new lids. Process for 5 minutes in boiling water bath. Makes 6 or 7 half-pints.

Garlic or Onion Butter
    5 stalks of wild onion or field garlic
    ½ lb. of butter or margarine
Wash the onion stalks and cut off any pieces that aren't nice. Soften the butter, and put butter and onions in the blender, blending until all the pieces disappear. The butter will take on a beautiful chartreuse color, and it tastes somewhat out of this world.

Pour the butter into a closeable plastic container and chill it. Serve as dip on crackers or French bread. Or slice French bread the long way, spread on the butter, and broil it a minute or two. Great!

Wild Onion Soup

¼ cup butter
1 cup of wild onions, sliced thin
1 Tbsp. flour
1 quart of beef stock

Melt butter in a skillet, add onions and saute until onions are clear yellow. Add flour and stir for 5 minutes. Add beef stock and simmer until onions are nice and tender. Serve with toast. Makes enough for four.

This next recipe is from Marie Mellinger, wild foods expert from Rabun County, Georgia. Once, at a meeting of the Florida Native Plant Society's Tarflower Chapter, I set up my camp stove and made this wild onion skillet bread. Everyone enjoyed it so much I couldn't make them fast enough!

Wild Onion Skillet Bread

1 ½ cups flour
1 ½ tsp. salt
½ cup cold water
1 cup wild onions, chopped

Mix ingredients together. Put a dollop of bacon fat in a skillet. When hot, drop the dough by tablespoonsful in the skillet and fry like pancakes.

Creamed Wild Onions

1 cup wild onions with leaves
1 Tbsp. butter
2 Tbsp. flour
¾ tsp. salt
Pepper to taste
1 cup milk

Wash onions thoroughly, remove tough skins from the outside, and any yellow parts from the leaves. Cut up into one-inch pieces. Simmer in water til tender. Melt butter, add flour, salt, and pepper, and cook, stirring, for a minute. Add onions, stir in milk, simmer until thick.

Wild Onions, Scrambled Eggs, and Bacon.
   6 wild onion bulbs, peeled, washed, and chopped
   4 slices of bacon
   2 Tbsp. milk
   2 eggs, beaten lightly
   Morton's Seasoned Salt to taste
   Fry bacon until almost crisp. Drain off fat except for 2 Tbsp. Push
bacon to one side of skillet. Add wild onions and seasoning salt, and
saute until onions are clear yellow. Remove bacon to plate. Add milk
to eggs in bowl, whip lightly. Add egg mixture to onions, and cook until
as done as you like them. Put eggs on top of bacon. Enjoy! I do, lots of
mornings!

   Here's another recipe from Marie Mellinger. This is a really
simple one. I haven't tried it, but when Marie does it, it's good.

   Clean and wash onions, parboil them, drain, cook them again, and
drain. Season with melted butter, dress with fried bread crumbs.

   And then there's this recipe. Just reading it sounds good.

Jelly Glazed Wild Onions
   ½ cup of beauty berry jelly
   1 Tbsp. butter
   20 wild onion bulbs
   Parboil the washed onions, and drain. Blend the jelly and butter
on low heat until smooth. Put onions in baking dish, add the jelly mix,
and bake for 20-30 minutes at 350°, turning several times until glazed.
Serves four.

The Ubiquitous Dandelion

A description of the ubiquitous dandelion (*Taraxacum officinale*) is hardly necessary. Whether
plant lovers or not, everyone
recognizes this common weed with
the basal rosette of long, deeply
toothed leaves, the head of yellow
florets, and the fluffy white ball of
seeds.

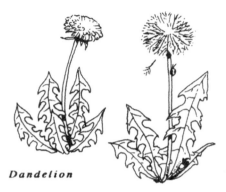

Dandelion

For ages, the dandelion has been known for its medicinal
properties all over the Old World and the Orient. Even the generic and
specific name, *Taraxacum officianale*, translates into "official
remedy for illnesses". The name dandelion means "the teeth of the
lion", but it's hard to decide if it's the golden "teeth" in the flowers, or
the "teeth" on the leaves.

I realize that the dandelion is not a native species, but it is
naturalized almost all over the United States. Its range extends into
Florida better than half way down the peninsula, and it is becoming
more and more prevalent in central Florida. When I moved to Orlando
32 years ago, it was hard to find. But now I think sod coming in from
just a little farther up the state is bringing it in and making it easier to
find.

The dandelion is another one of the completely useful wild edibles.
I like the ones that can be used totally. The only part of the dandelion
that is not edible is the hollow flower stem.

The best known part of the plant is the high-vitamin greens. When
they are young and tender they can be used for salad greens. If they get
a little bitter as they age, mix them with other salad greens. Some
authors say that the fresh greens should be covered with boiling water,
then rinsed to remove some of the bitter taste, and chilled before using
as a salad. Others say the bitter taste is desirable. Cold weather

sweetens the leaves.

When they become too bitter to eat raw, you can boil them in one or more changes of water. Add butter or bacon grease and enjoy as a cooked vegetable. In France they eat cooked dandelion greens between slices of buttered bread.

Another good way to prepare them is to finely chop a half cup of fresh tender leaves and mix them into a half pint of sour cream for a dip. Fresh chopped leaves also can be added to pancake or fritter batter.

Next, let's take into consideration the crown of the dandelion. This is the part of the plant that is light colored, just above the tap root from which emerge the leaves and flowers. This can be cut from the root, washed, stripped of the leaves and flower buds (for use later), and boiled for only a couple of minutes. Then saute in butter and serve with your favorite dressing.

The young roots of dandelion can be scrubbed and boiled for about 20 minutes in salted water, then sliced and served with butter and a dash of hot sauce. The roots can also be roasted in a 250-degree oven until crackly-dry and golden-brown all the way through. Grind and use for a coffee substitute or extender. You may also add some roasted and ground persimmon seeds for an interesting drink. Ground roasted chicory root can also be added. Dandelion roots can be dug and used at any time of the year.

Now let's see what we can do to prepare the buds for eating. Like the crown from which they emerge, the buds should be cooked only a couple of minutes, drained, and served with butter and a dash of lemon. The buds are also very tasty when pickled.

The flowers can be dipped in a batter of flour, beaten egg, milk, salt, and pepper, then fried, and dipped in salt to serve as an appetizer (recipe by Marie Mellinger). Care must be taken to remove all the stem parts from the flowers in any of their uses because the stems are bitter, bitter, bitter!

The blossoms are also used to make wine, and there are a great number of recipes for wine-making. But my good friend, Gail Beck, from just outside of Dillard, Georgia, has a recipe for a dandelion soft drink (non-alcoholic) that is fantastic.

Fill a quart measure firmly with fresh dandelion blossoms. Rinse and cut off stems very close to the flower heads. Cover with 2 quarts of boiling water and set aside to cool.

Combine 2 cups of cold water with 3 cups of sugar and bring to a boil to make 3 cups of syrup.

Thinly slice 2 lemons and 2 oranges. Add them and the syrup to the flowers, and let stand for 2 to 3 days. Strain and serve over cracked ice. To keep longer, the strained mixture may be bottled and corked tightly, or should be refrigerated. Makes two quarts of a healthful, non-intoxicating drink.

Hawk's beard

Besides the "real" dandelion (*Taraxacum officinale*), there are a couple more dandelion types — some that you're more likely to find throughout Florida — that can be used for salads and cooked greens when gathered at a very young stage of growth. They are false dandelion (*Pyrrhopappus carolinianus*) and hawk's beard (*Youngia japonica* syn. *Crepis japonica*). I first found the common name of hawk's beard in Walter Taylor's book, *Guide to Florida Wildflowers*. You must be able to recognize these plants before the flower stalks appear. Once in flower they are much too bitter.

As far as nutrition goes, dandelions are better than any of our garden vegetables (which are bred for easy harvest, beautiful color and appearance, resistance to disease, and to mature all at the same time, etc). The whole dandelion plant contains an impressive list of vitamins and minerals, especially the leaves.

False dandelion

This is another of the weeds you can find in your yard, and if you don't like it growing in your lawn, eat it!

Potato Substitutes

The list of plants whose roots, tubers, corms, and bulbs can be used as substitutes for potatoes is not as extensive as those plants that can serve as salads or potherbs, but they are nonetheless useful and important. Most of these potato substitutes can be used in recipes calling for potatoes.

Some of them can be gathered any time of the year, but most should be gathered in late fall, winter, and early spring, for this is the time when the plant stores its energy for the next year's growth. In the fall and winter this energy is mostly in the form of starch. In the early spring the stored starch starts to turn to sugar for the start of the new growth. If you like your "potatoes" a little starchy, gather in the fall and all winter. If you like them a little sweeter, gather in early spring.

Harvest only what you need for the immediate time, for most of these tubers do not store very well. Naturally, they all must be washed thoroughly before using. As with the Irish potato, the skin should be left on most tubers in preparation, because most of the "goodies" — that is, the vitamins and minerals — are in the layer just under the skin.

Jerusalem artichoke or sunchoke (*Helianthus tuberosus*). The sunchoke, a tuberous sunflower, is a coarse plant, up to about eight feet tall and rough to the touch. Both the disks and the ray flowers are yellow, and about three inches across. Each flower has 9 to 15

Sunchoke

rays. The leaves are alternate, ovate, and tapering to a point. The upper part of the plant is well branched with flowers on the end of almost every branch.

You need to observe all this, and remember where the patch of sunchokes are, because the winter die-back is complete. There may be some remnants of the stems, but most of the dead leaves will have been stripped away by the wind. If you break off one of the dead stems, you should find a pure white pith inside. This is a good indicator that you will find the tubers if you dig.

Sunchoke is native only in the central United States, but it has been extensively cultivated and has escaped almost throughout Florida. The Indians used it as a trade item, further dispersing it.

The tubers contain a carbohydrate called inulin, which is digestible by people who can't digest other starches. Besides being used as a potato substitute, sunchoke can be eaten raw, sliced into a salad, or pickled, making it one of the very best wild foods. It is also one of the few wild foods that have been exported to Europe.

Sunchoke is also one of the few tubers that store well — for months — in the refrigerator, if it is harvested in the spring just before the new sprouts start to grow.

Water shield (*Brasenia schreberi*) is another of the water lily types that has small tubers that can be harvested and prepared like potatoes, but this plant was not included in the chapter on Water Lilies. These plants, including spatterdock, yellow pond lily, and the American lotus, are the exceptions to the suggestion to leave on the peels when preparing them to eat, for their thick outer skins are unpalatable (see chapter on Water Lilies).

Arrowhead or Duck Potatoes (*Sagittaria* spp.). Several different species, all called arrowheads, produce tubers. All of them are always found in wet places — pond and stream edges — making it necessary for the forager to get wet. Most of the tubers are on thin roots some distance from the plant stems.

The Indians used arrowhead potatoes, and collecting the tubers was the job of the Indian women. They held onto the gunwale of a canoe and stomped around in the mud to kick the tubers free with their feet. When the tubers floated to the surface of the water, the women put them into the canoe. That technique still works as well as it did a hundred years ago, but you can also scrape the mud near the plants with a rake or hoe until the tubers surface.

The leaves of *Sagittaria* may be arrowhead-shaped, elliptic (broadest in the middle and tapering to both ends), or they may be grass-like.

The tubers can be prepared any way you would prepare a potato. They are not tasty raw, but boiled, roasted, or baked, they are worth the trouble of gathering them!

Groundnuts (*Apios americana*). A wide-spreading vining legume, groundnut has smooth, green, compound leaves with five to seven egg-shaped leaflets tapered to a point. Its clusters of pea-shaped, maroon to brown flowers are very fragrant and originate from the leaf axils. It grows in damp places.

The root produces a string of fleshy tubers not very deep in the soil. The Indians

Groundnut

considered these tubers an excellent food. Prepare them any way you do potatoes, boiled, or sliced and fried. hey are very tasty, but eat them while they are still warm — they're not good cold. They're expecially good in stir-fried meals.

Groundnut vines also produce beans, which are edible when shelled and cooked.

Evening Primrose (*Oenothera biennis*). The first year, evening primrose produces only a rosette of leaves flat on the ground. The second year the plant sends up a flower spike with many yellow flowers. Fall and winter of the first year is when the tap root of this plant is edible.

After digging up the root, cook it in two changes of boiling water; otherwise it is much too spicey. Then mash it, remove the fibers, and eat the remaining "mashed potatoes".

The flowers are also edible out of hand, or as a vegetable, boiled and buttered, but if you eat the root of the first year, of course there will be no flowers the second.

Daylily (*Hemerocallis fulva*). The daylily is such a common garden plant with its orange flowers that I don't think any further description is necessary.

Daylily is another one of the many-purpose plants. The firm, young tubers can be scrubbed and eaten raw or sliced onto a salad, as well as cooked as a potato. The buds can be cooked like green beans. The fully-opened flower petals can be added to a salad. Withered flowers make a good addition to a soup or stew, or flowers can be dried and stored for later use as a thickener for soups and stews. The plant also yields a yellow dye.

Wild Potato Vine (*Ipomoea pandurata*). This morning glory vine is sometimes called "man of the earth". This is the *only* morning glory with an edible root and it should *not* be eaten raw. Its leaves are heart-shaped and its flowers are typical morning glory shape — white with a pinkish-purple throat. The enormous root of this spiraling vine goes straight down into the ground.

Boil the root in two changes of water.

Air Potato (*Dioscorea bulbifera*). A climbing, sprawling vine, air potato will cover all other vegetation if not kept in check. It's not a native to Florida, but comes from tropical Asia, and does not bloom here.

It has large, heart-shaped leaves, and produces air tubers from pea size to about three inches in diameter that are *not* edible. Every one of those little tubers, unfortunately, has the potential for starting a new huge vine, even if you cut them up and throw them on the trash pile. If you have one of these vines in your area, destroy the air tubers by putting them in a dark plastic bag and tying the top shut until they rot! Then, follow the vine back to its origin and dig down. You will find an enormous root that is edible like a potato. Boil it in two changes of water, and then slice it, or mash it, or bake it in a casserole with cheese, or chill it and make salad.

Tread Softly or Spurge Nettle (*Cnidoscolus stimulosus*). I was advised to not include tread softly because it is so nasty to handle and the tubers are deep, but the taste is excellent and it is available throughout the year.

All the parts above the ground have stinging hairs, even the flowers. The flowers are white, tubular with five lobes, and they are armed! The leaves are dark green, deeply lobed, toothed, alternate — and armed!

The stem (also armed) goes some distance down into the ground, then thins out to string size. You follow the string down in the ground to find the tubers, which come in all shapes and sizes up to two feet long! The best way to excavate them, I have found, is to dig down beside the plant with posthole diggers or a shovel, and pull the tubers out from the side.

Just take care not to touch any of the plant parts above ground. If you do, I've been told that rubbing it with crushed dock leaves — which often grows nearby — will help neutralize the stinging agent.

Boil the tubers for about 20 minutes, or until soft, in slightly salted water. Drain them, and mash them through a screen or food mill to remove the fibers, and then serve with butter like mashed potatoes.

INDEX

Page numbers in **bold** indicate first page of chapter on topic.

Achillea millefolium, 45
acorns, **27**
air potato, 65
Allium spp., 9, **55**
almonds, 32
amaranth, 8, 13
Amaranthus spp., 8, 13
American lotus, 49
Apios americana, 64
arbor vitae, 46
arrowhead, 63

basket oak, 27
basswood, 32, 46
bear grass, 8
beauty berry, **24**
beautybush, 24
bed straw, 13
beechnuts, 32
beer, 38
beverages, 18, 37, 39, **42**, 44, 52, 53, 60, 61
Bidens alba, 9, 13
biscuits, 33, 34, 53
bitter cress, 8
black drink, 42
black oak, 26
black walnut, 18, 30
blackberry, 43
blaspheme vine, 8
blue beech, 32
blue lettuce, 13
bracken fern, 8
Brasenia schreberi, 63
Brassica spp., 8, 13
bread, 18, 28, 34, 49, 57
bullrush, 8

cactus, **52**
Cakile spp., 8, 13
Callicarpa americana, **24**
camphor tree, 37, 44
cancer jalap, 14
candy, 22, 29, 47, 53
Capsella bursa-pastoris, 9, 13
Cardamine pennsylvanica, 8, 13
Carpinus caroliniana, 32
carving, 19
Carya spp., 30
cashew family, 20
casserole, 12, 34
Castanea spp., 31
catbriar, 8
cattail, 4, 8, **33**
Cercis canadensis, 8
champagne, 40, 47
Chenopodium spp., 13, 46

chicory, 47, 60
chickweed, 6, 8, 13
chinquapins, 31
chocolate substitute, 46
Chrysanthemum leucanthemum, 8
chufa, 46, 47
Cichorium intybus, 47
Cinnamomum camphora, 44
Cirsium spp., 9
cleavers, 8
clover, 13, 44, 47
Cnidoscolus stimulosus, 66
coconut, 32
Cocos nucifera, 32
coffee substitutes, See beverages
Commelina spp., 8, 13
cookies, 38, 49
Corylus americana, 31
cow oak, 27
creeping mint, 7, 8, 43
curly dock, 13
Cyperus esculentus, 46, 47

Dahoon holly, 42
dandelion, 6, 8, 13, 16, 47, **59**
Daucus carota, 13
dayflower, 6, 8, 13
daylily, 8, 65
dewberry, 43
Dioscorea bulbifera, 65
Diospyros virginiana, **17**, 44
dock, 16
dollarweed, 13
drinks, See beverages
duck potatoes, 63
dye, 16, 31, 65

earth almond, 46
Eichhornia crassipes, 13
elderberry, **39**, 47
Erechtites hieracifolia, 8, 13
evening primrose, 64
exports, 14, 63

Fagus grandifolia, 32
false dandelion, 8, 13, 61
fir, 46
fireweed, 8, 13
Florida betony, 5, 8, **10**
flour, 28, 33, 49, 51
French mulberry, **24**
fruit leather, 18

galinsoga, 13
Galinsoga ciliata, 13
Galium spp., 8, 13
garget, 14

INDEX

garlic, **55**
garlic or onion butter, 56
gill-over-the-ground, 43
glasswort, 8
Glechoma hederacea, 43
goldenrod, 42, 43
grape, 5, 8
greenbriar, 8, 13
greens, **5, 11,** 61
ground ivy, 43
groundnuts, 64

hamburgers, 29
hawk's beard, 13, 61
hazelnut, 31
Helianthus tuberosus, 8, 62
Hemerocallis fulva, 8, 65
hemlock, 46
henbit, 13, 32
herbicides, 4
hickory, 30
hollies, 42
hornbeam, 32
horsebriar, 8
Hydrocotyle spp., 13

ice cream, 17
Ilex spp. 42
ink, 15
inkberry, 14
insecticides, 4
Ipomoea pandurata, 65

jelly, 15, 22, 25, 38, 39, 53, 58
Jerusalem artichoke, 2, 8, 24, 62
Juglans nigra, 30

Lactuca spp., 9, 13
lamb's quarters, 13
Lamium amplexicaule, 13, 43
laurel family, 36,
laurel oak, 27
laxative, 15
Lepidium virginicum, 8
lily family, 55
lotus, 49

malic acid, 20, 45
meadow garlic, 55
meadow beauty, 8
medicinal, 43
Mentha spp., 8, 43
Mexican tea, 46
Micromeria brownei, 7, 8, 43
minerals, 3, 7, 61, 62
mint, 8, 42, 43, 47
Mitchella repens, 8
mockernut, 30

monkey lice, 9
morning glory vine, 65
muffins, 28, 49
mustard, 8, 13, 16, 55

ñamoli, 14
Nelumbo lutea, 49
Nuphar lutea, 49
nut grass, 46
nutrition, 3
nuts, 3, 30, 46
Nymphaea odorata, 49
Nymphaeaceae, 49

oaks, 27
Oenothera biennis, 64
onions, **55**
Opuntia spp., **52**
Oxalis spp., 6, 9
oxeye daisy, 8

pancakes, 18, 28, 33, 39, 53, 60
Parietaria floridana, 8
partridge berry, 8
pecan, 30
pellitory, 8
Pennsylvania cress, 13
pennyroyal, 43
peppergrass, 5, 6, 8, 16, 55
peppermint, 43
Persea spp., 36, 55
persimmon, 3, **17,** 42, 47, 60
pesticides, 12
Phytolacca americana, 13, **14**
pickerel weed, 8, 13
pickles, 10, 16, 34, 55, 56, 60, 63
pie, 15, 40
pigeon berry, 14
pignut hickory, 30
Piloblephis rigida, 43
pine, 31, 46
Pinus spp., 31, 46
Plantago major, 8, 13
plantain, 8, 13
pocan, 14
poison ivy, 23
poison sumac, 23, 44
poisonous plants, 14, 15, 23, 26, 44
poke, 3, 13, **14**
poke sallet, 14
pokeberry, 14
pokeweed, 14
pollutants, 4, 6
pond lily, 49
Pontederia cordata, 8, 13
Portulaca oleracea, 8, 13
potato substitutes, **62**
Pteridium aquilinum, 8

INDEX

purslane, 6, 8, 13
Pyrrhopappus carolinianus, 8, 13, 61

quallah, 21
Queen Anne's lace, 13
Quercus spp., **27**

radish, **10**
red cedar, 46
red oak, 27
red bud, 8
redroot pigweed, 13
redweed, 14
redwood, 14
Rhexia virginica, 8
Rhus spp., 20, 21, 44
Rosa spp., 9, 45
rosehip tea, 45
roses, 45
Rubus spp., 43
Rumex spp., 8, 13

Sagittaria spp., 63
salad greens, **5**, 44, 59, 61, 63, 65
Salicornia spp., 8
Sambucus canadensis, **39**, 47
sandspurs, 2
sassafras, **36**, 44
Sassafras albidum, **36**, 44
saw palmetto, 8
Scirpus validus, 8
scoke, 14
scrub hickory, 30
sea rocket, 8, 13
Serenoa repens, 8
sheep sorrel, 6, 8, 13
shepherd's purse, 9, 13
Smilax spp., 5, 8, 13
soft drink, 61
Solidago odora 43
Sonchus spp., 9, 13
soups and stews, 38, 49, 51, 53, 54, 57, 65
sow thistle, 9, 13
Spanish bayonet, 9
Spanish needle, 9, 13
spatterdock, 50
spearmint, 43
spiderwort, 9, 13
spinach, 11
spiny amaranth, 13
spruce, 46
spurge nettle, 66
Stachys floridana, 8, **10**
Stellaria media, 8, 13

sumac, **20**, 44
sunchoke, 62
sunflower, 24, 62
supermarkets, 14, 37, 43, 52
swamp chestnut oak, 27
swamp rose, 9
syrup, 47, 53

tannic acid, tannin, 20, 27, 28
Taraxacum officinale, 8, 13, 47, **59**
tea, See beverages
thirst-quencher, 24, 61
thistle, 9
Tilia americana, 32, 46
tobacco, 21
torches, 35
Toxicodendron spp., 23
Tradescantia ohiensis, 9, 13
tread softly, 66
Trifolium spp., 13, 44
tubers, 10, 46, 49, 62
turkey oak, 27
Typha spp., 8, 33
verbena family, 24
Viola spp., 9, 13, 44, 47
violet, 9, 13, 44, 47
Virginia willow, 24
vitamins, 3, 6, 7, 45, 59, 61, 62
Vitis spp., 8

walnut, 30
water cress, 5, 6
water hickory, 30
water hyacinth, 13
water lilies, **49**
water pennywort, 13
water shield, 63
water pennywort, 13
white oak, 27
wild garlic, 9, **55**
wild lettuce, 9
wild onion, 9, **55**
wild potato vine, 65
wine, 15, 40, 47, 60
wood, 19, 37
wood sorrel, 9

yarrow tea, 45
yaupon, 42
yellow nut grass, 47
yellow lettuce, 13
yellownut sedge, 46
youngia, 9, 13, 61
Youngia japonica, 9, 13, 61
Yucca spp., 8, 9